ART OF HUMOR

HOW PEOPLE JOKE WITH EACH OTHER

- Nicholas Santa Clore -

Copyright © 2020 Nicholas Santa Clore

All rights reserved. No part of this book may be reproduced or transmitted in any form or by any means, electronic or mechanical, including photo- copying, recording, or by any information storage and retrieval system, except in the case of brief quotations embodied in critical articles and reviews, without prior written permission of the publisher.

Contents

**CHAPTER I: WHAT IS HUMOR?** ............ 7
   WHAT IS HUMOR ............ 7
   WHY DID I DECIDE TO WRITE THIS BOOK   8
   THE FEATURE OF HUMOR ............ 11
   THE CONDITIONS OF HUMOR ............ 21

**CHAPTER II: HOW TO DO IT** ............ 30
   THE POPULAR METHOD OF JOKE ............ 31
   THIS WAY IS BASICALLY ............ 37
   A VERY SELDOM WAY ............ 48
   THE DIRTY WAY ............ 58
   A VERY HOT WAY ............ 76
   A VERY HARD WAY ............ 87
   A VERY CHARMING WAY ............ 95
   A VERY COMPLICATED WAY ............ 105

**CHAPTER III: FIDDLE-FADDLE** ............ 120
   SOME BASIC ADVISE ............ 122
   HUMAN ESSENTIAL ............ 125
   BENEFIT OF SMILING ............ 131
   HUMOR AND LOVE ............ 134
   HUMOROUS TOOLS ............ 136
   HOW TO SUCESS FROM CHUCKLE WITH THIS BOOK ............ 142

## INTRODUCTION

In reality, Mostly people in the world don't know how to joke effectively, Joke Or humor By themself is something hard to teach and describe to others!

Worse, so many people misunderstand humor or making joke is saying something rude or hurting others feeling by ridiculing the disadvantages of their friends, then very few of them know clearly about it, For trying to make people in the world understand about joke or humor, this book is born to do these missions, this book was written because of a long time in experience working as a tourist guide, and a long time traveling around the country interacting with different people from different continents: Asia, America, Europe, Oceania..., it made me found out Humor rules and it has no border, even though languages, cultures is a barrier but having the same rules, this book also born from my luck of

# ART OF HUMOR

living in a village that surrounding me are funny people from my father, my mother, my uncle, my friends ... the experience of learning the funny tips from them made me happy every day, this book is a result of a long time learning and practicing the funny things in Society, then I may consider it as an act of saving the world from boring, sadness and frustrated If you read this book effectively

The book including 2 chapters with different contents, the first chapter a little boring and sleepy with researching of a joke under academic views, I consider it as a basis of humor, the second chapter maybe will wake you up with so many tips for a joke but please do not skip the chapter because lack of any knowledge in this book may lead to unpredictable consequences…

Now let's start this book with your hand holding a cup of coffee…

NICHOLAS SANTA CLORE

Hopefully, the world will become funnier every single day, and hopefully after reading this book, in someone's eyes, you are not perfect but you are funny!

## CHAPTER I: WHAT IS HUMOR?

WHAT IS HUMOR

What is an awkward question but indeed one of the factors of humor is something awkward people will smile when something awkward, they different to the common things, it seems to be lack of something to make it easier to understand, for answering this question, finding some information on the internet, and this is the way how Wikipedia tells us about Humor :

"Humour (British English), also spelled as humor (American English), is the tendency of experiences to provoke laughter and provide Amusement. The term derives from the Humoral medicine of the ancient Greeks, which taught that the balance of fluids in the human body, known as humours (Latin: *humor*, "body fluid"), controlled human health and emotion."

hmm... So complicated! for me, humor is Simpler, It is capable to make other people smile, laugh by somehow!

## WHY DID I DECIDE TO WRITE THIS BOOK

In a long time of learning people that having a good sense of humor, I found out all of them having the same points, there are 3 things that I got from them: Good IQ and EQ, they have a habit of using language in humor, they have a well capable of emotional expression, these factors playing an important role for making someone have a good sense of humor, without one of them, joke become distorted and rudeness, in that each of them have an important role such as:

**1.** good IQ and EQ: IQ(Intelligent Quote) the person having this factor from medium level will have a well capable of summarizing data, information in the purpose of a joke

EQ(Emotional Quote) This factor Playing more important role than the last one, the person having good EQ will know when is the most suitable time for saying something funny or not, it also decided factor in humor

2. good habit of using language: so many people have a good sense of humor having their habitual style in communication, The experience of funny speech in the past created their habits of using the language for humor if you pay attention the funny person or comedians sometimes they talking in seriousness but we still feeling something funny emanate from them, these habits may come from their social influence or a long period of practicing, indeed they are habits, and humor habits are diversity, for example, the humor style of Kevin Hart is different to Mr. Bean, also each culture have it own humor style, this book will show you the most basic styles that

people used in the world and when we apply it, in reality, it will work in any culture, language, verbal or non-verbal language,mainly the mission of this book is focus on humor habits and creating humor habits is your mission!

3. Good capable of emotional expression: this is a less important factor than two last I mentioned to, however lack of this factor, it is similar to a soup lacking a little spice, still delicious but not perfect, the next chapter will explain why this factor having an important role. I recognize the second and the third factor above by learning and practicing, one person might improve the sense of humor by following the humor rules in every chapter of this book, the first factor depending on yourself with the capability of controlling your own emotion

Another factor to make something fun is the audience, I believe each people having a little humor in them but some of them don't know how to interpret it and to understand and laugh to a humor signal, the audience needs to have a little humor in them, it similar to communication in machines (an output device need an input device), improving audience also the mission of this book, hopefully! Moreover, humor may an endowment or learned is not important, the most important is humor skills if you misunderstand this book is for teaching good communication.

THE FEATURE OF HUMOR

Further, analyze of humor we may see that it's the combination of many factors they're: simply things, lively, fast in reaction, academic, generous

- ***Simply things***. Humor by itself really simply, remember the last thing in your mind that makes you smile..., yes it is! Our brain reacts to other factors fast so smiling at any moment needing simple action or simply speech, if you want to do the humor with complicated action or speech, that's good, but the audience's face may twist then they ask you the question "hey! What's going on?" This question will force you to explain your action or speech

There is nothing failure than explaining your joke to audience, then they(the audience )will "ha ha ha" at you with a donated laugh.

Most people in the world love the IOS operating system of Apple because everything of Apple so simple and easier to understand for all people in the world when I'm writing this book at this moment Apple still simply with IOS 12, but I'm not sure when you reading this book it's still simply or not, but this example shows that something with essential simplicity usually more effective than a complicated one, we usually see that people having a good sense of humor mostly having capable of using language in concise and simple word, the simplicity was seen in parody, comedy or stories from stand up comedian with simply film script ( Johnny English, Beverly Hills Ninja, The Great Dictator…), it also similar to merit of generous people, most of them having simply thinking with simple ideas then humor is a characteristic we usually see in them, right now some of you may disagree with me about this point of view because humor included much more than I say, that's right!

there are more merit and language habit will be shown next pages because humor essential is abstraction these points of view showing it in simplicity, this part will be closed with Leonardo Da Vinci's quote "Simplicity is the ultimate sophistication"

- *Fast of reaction:*

humor can be a skill to solve any problem in your whole life, at first you need some ability of humor that need for a joke, in this feature if you having a capacity of fast in reaction in every situation, that's your hallow, it's a good potential of creating humor, however fast in the reaction is not enough, it needs a little technique such as an answer or saying something in a suitable way, I remembered a show of live concert in Russia 2012, the show was live on television with over 1000 audiences watching it, the Master of the ceremony (MC) is introducing the next song then suddenly the stage was collapsed,the Mc strongly fall over of the stage, it makes the crowd were upset and panic, immediately the mc guy suddenly stand up *"Do you feel it ok?, I have practiced this fall hit for three months!"* - he said, The crowd laughed out loud with applause, he continued: the next song belongs to our staff with the song of cleaning!! Staff after that come out with applause from audiences,this example show us that fast of reaction and a suitable speech can turn the situation from failure into victory,if the MC say *"wtf"* or *"oh my god", "jesus cry..."* the situation may become worse,through the reaction of the MC we see that it suitable with his situation,the fast of reaction impact to our brain with impression and surprising,they are the important factors that lead to smile or laugh,Charlie chapin an icon of fast in reaction,in the beginning of his career,his film was did with uncomplete film script such as City Lights(1931), Modern Time (1936), The Gold Rush (1925) alway working the ideal out on film as ideas were accept or not,a narrative structure would emerge that depend on his reaction,it also frame the film from the beginning,we recognize that good script doesn't plan before,it come from his natural reaction it require his humor work naturally,once again fast of reaction play an important role in humor,we can see this feature in every humor person,such as an event was happened in 1987 the US president Ronal Reagan was visited Germany for Celebration of Berlin 750th anniversary,right here he had a speech in public, all the corner of palace were decorated with colorful balloons and full of animated crowd,when Reagan having speech in public,a balloon suddenly popped up very loudly, it similar to someone attempting to assassinate the US President,in that moment,Reagan just stopped his speech in 1 second and replied in calm: *"Missed me!"*

This fast reaction was made the crowd laugh out loud with applause because all people were thought Reagan may duck under his table with panic, also a man with his personality is cuteness having this capable of fast in reaction always make people around him surprising, the key of humor comes from this merit, are you cuteness person? If you say yes this is the good chance to improve your joke in reading this book if you say no, keep heading to the next parts maybe you may find your merit from it

- *Lively*

It seems to be awkward when I put lively as a feature of humor but it's work effectively when we apply it in communication, you may absolutely agree to me when you know two or three languages, humor by it essential not depend on language we are using but funny idea, language is the transportation of funny idea, indeed from the funny idea we can understand the comedy from other countries other cultures with or without subtitle, so language by itself is a small part in humor(paronomasia), also mostly human brain was reminded the past by broken fragment images so When you try to describe something in any language really lively, the capable of making impression and joke always better than non-lively speech, so impacting directly to audience imagination by your language will make it work, cause why people smile

### *Impacting directly to the imagination*

if you pay attention to novel of J.K Rowling ,lively also the technique that she attract the readership In the whole world by her fictional novel Harry Potter, The technique was used to describe some particular characters such as Dursley couple: *"he was a big,beefy man with hardly any neck, although he have a very large mustache, Mrs Dursley was thin and blonde and had nearly twice the usual amount of neck which came in very useful as she spent So much of her time craning over garden fences spying on the neighborhoods"* The lively words also used by so many famous stand up comedians,about 70% of Comedy show with lively words have been used, lively in body language in the way of expressing emotion, telling some stories in the past by simulating the situation and characters is a common style of funny story,describing action or speech happened in the past,reviving true story then forcing audiences open their imagination in lively pictures,let's think of mr Bean with a flexible face from Rowan Atkinson or the rebel of your lover on the bed, i'm sure that all pictures were summarized in your mind with a lively imagination

- *Academic*

The academic joke, Yes! You do not misunderstand meThis situation will happen when somebody having the same job or living the same environment with others in the period of communication, people joke by using jargon, this phenomenon mostly was created because of occupational disease, instead of using common words, speakers will use the jargon to talk with each other for their habit, Sometime for the purpose of coding they communication to avoid other people know it directly, this method of communication will force human brain take a lot of time to encode jargon to normal meaning,the period of encoding jargon will impress human brain that lead to intense feeling,a cause of making someone smile,that's the reason why I set it as one of humor features, imagination you and your colleague code the conversation by jargon other people may look at you like alien people, an example prove this humor factor work effectively ,it's an event that happened in White House 2014, when the former president of the United States of America Barack Obama in a speech of new technology in US Army, He said "basically, I'm here to announce that we're building iron man" the crowd were laugh out loud after that,although he immediately confessed that *"I'm blast off for a second"* it cannot keep people laughing louder,now we see that it(academic joke) just only work when you are American or fan of marvel Dc comic,many people know it because marvel Dc comic very popular in America,then Iron man is jargon, if you are not American or worser not a fan of Marvel you may confuse with some question such as why do they laugh? What is he talking about? Who is Iron Man, Obama is crazy! Etc... , in conclusion, this method usually uses in a closed society where people only understand with each other by coding conversations, it is also the most complicated feature,then it is not so popular, people using it fewer in common life!

- ***Generous***

Most of the people can joke having it, if you got this merit I'm sure that you are a little bit humor, this merit takes the person having an opener mind then it will create space for creation, I call it as a free open mind, especially generous people had no caring to the little things so the trouble cannot catch them, a good way to become happier and bring happiness to the other by funny things, I remember a blogger very success on the internet as a nickname Paubyerly, he is the master of the blog themarriagebed.com, he recognized himself as a generous man, faced to a question *"how is a generous man?"* he commented: *"am I generous? I supposed I had better be given, I have been writing a daily blog called " The generous husband For 16 years, but in all honesty, I have learned to be generous from my wife who is a master of it"* this comment was recognized as the best answer on Quora with the little awkward internal question, also this factor(generous)will break the limit inside your mind for creating new things, the person having this virtue mostly having the capable of joking other people but also having the capability of joking themself,for a generous person, they usually not consider somethings so important because when they consider something too important it may create the nervous and think too much, that make humor and the funny things gone, moreover The optimistic spirit makes them feel better in every situation, so I consider generous is the original of humor and generous is important for humor, in the next chapter I will show you the most way to being funny, it's implying, the person that have not this merit (generous), they may distort humor by saying cruel implying, It's very hard to become an angel but for becoming the monster, it just takes some second! So to be happy just generous!

THE CONDITIONS OF HUMOR

If you are reading this book I am sure that sometime you have tried to joke someone but you fail, it is may make you embarrassing and you may never want to do it anymore, my first advice does not try to joke someone when you feeling uncomfortable, for the success joke we need the first impression, it will create the friendly environment to improve the relationship of speakers and audiences ( in this book I try to not use the word "joker" word because it may obsess readership because of evil joker in cinema )

The first impression working as a flywheel, when you do something success at first, your flywheel start running, and the next period of communication become more smoothly and easier to create the interesting things, but what happens if you can not make the first impression, your flywheel not work, for this case, if you lose confidence, you fail, the game is over, otherwise you still keeping it(confidence) internal, there are 3 levels of audiences mental we need to pay attention for success in a joke:

- **Easy**

In this mental level mostly audiences having good mental status, they may be having a good day, the smile is blowing on their lips, the facial muscles are stretching then your flywheel may start to run easier for the first impression, there are 3 signs of success joke from low to high: chuckle, smile, and laugh, in this mental level you joke someone with a very lame story or little awkward act, the audience having the tendency of smiling and laughter, the sign of chuckle is very seldom(the dotted line in chart), in this case, all your failure in communication will be dismissed by the audience but please note that do not go too far, do not try to joke to their taboos such as political views, cultural disadvantages, their fashion or working style, in this mental level, the speaker should use the basic way of a joke they are surprising, implying, comparison, emotional expression that I will show you in the next chapter, so please don't be hurry keep calm and waiting for the next chapter!

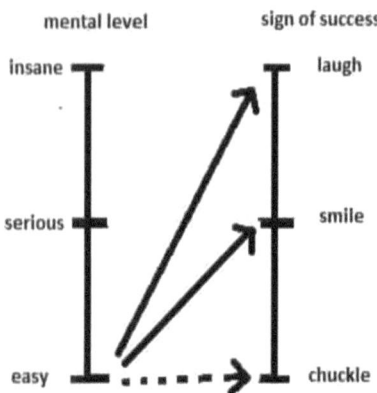

- **Serious** :

in this mental level, it's become harder to joke someone, for this case our audience may having 2 kinds: the crowd(public) and personal, for the crowd from 10 people or crowder, it's easier to joke them even though they are keeping the seriousness on their face, a joke in public will succeed with a little awkward, a little lame, the public may smile or laugh because the funny effect will spread in the crowd, I call it is the resonant frequency, but to do this as the success joke, you should be a confident speaker on the stage or in front of a crowd, because so many eyes are watching you every step, every action, every movement of your facial muscle have its own meaning, For the public joking, some methods I recommend you to use in front of a crowd, they are surprising, trending speech, emotional expression and most popular Is implying, These necessary techniques, of course, will be shown in the next chapter, so please do not hurry, keep calm and wait for the next chapter! For the speakers or artists of success in a joke, most of them having the best skill of pretending to be serious, they can say something awkward with a serious face, this is the deciding factor to joke someone success or not, Moreover, for a successful joke in conversation it's included a paradox of joke, this paradox is a sign to imply that you are joking, the paradox will be described in the chart below:

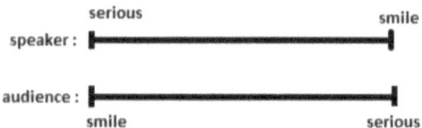

Its meaning is " when you joke someone, it's obligate to have a funny sign from speaker or audience in the period of conversation if the audience not smile the speaker needs to joke with a chuckle, the best way to save the speaker from tough situations, it sends to the audience a message: I just joke, let's chill, Barack Obama is well known as a funny president of America, his speech usually make the audiences laugh, sometimes the audiences not laugh, his joke doesn't work He also crack himself in public, the best way to avoid embarrassing for a president, we can find this moment easily on YouTube today with the keyword "Obama crack himself up" then the audience smile, speaker's face turn back to serious, so trust me, making a joke is the art of pretending to be serious.

For making a joke in personal communication when the audience having a serious mental level, the speaker should find out the cause of their mood, serious mood also the common attitude in communication, for this case, we should apply the gentle joke such as implying, emotional expression or comparison, limit for mocking someone in this mental level, the speaker also apply the joke paradox in this case, the sign of success for this case mostly are chuckling or smiling but if you do the best, laughing is the sign that proves you are brilliant

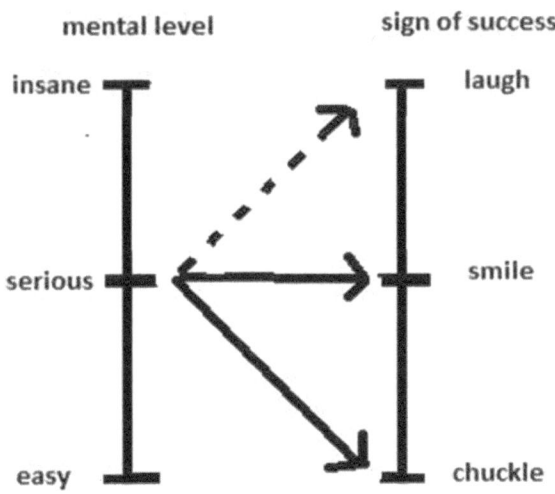

- insane:

In this book the word "insane" have the different meaning than common,it's not indicate crazy it's for describing a mental level only ,This mental level showing that the audience in extreme situation,they may have some problems internal: disappointment,sad,anger,nervous or stressful… in this case,the speaker need to find out the causing of their mental,this step will decide your capable of joke, your joke right now not only for the purpose of fun but also for sympathy,my tip for this case is finding and magnifying the optimistic side of their problem,proving that they were lucky with tough situation by using quotes,trending speech,this method will inspire the audience escape from their miserableness, 3 years ago i led a group of traveler with about 15 people most of them are young boys, we were trekking on a mountain together in a drizzle day, the trail is A little bit slippery and suddenly a boy( his name Jason) has fallen as slide down of muddy, immediately his friend who went after him yell : "*no pain no gain ! Jason! Are you alive?*" Jason, after that stand up with a smile on his face he keeps walking and mumbling "*no pain no gain no pain again*" since that time I recognize that the quotes having a massive power, then I applied it for so many situations and having the same miserableness such as:

- the boy was fallen in practicing bicycle: no pain no gain!

- The young girl knocked her head again the door: no pain, no gain

# ART OF HUMOR

- For the man cannot persuade his bunch of friends to drink wine while they only want to drink beer: if you cannot beat them join them

All the case will become success joke in the condition of quotes suitable with their situation, all your joke have to start from your heart with sympathy, For this level of mental the success sign of joke is chuckling, imagination a man with heavy sorrow and gloomy face suddenly chuckle because of your joke, I consider it as a victory!

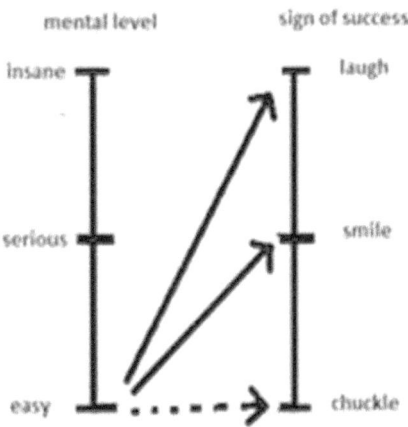

## *CHAPTER II: HOW TO DO IT*

In this chapter I will show you some basic ways to joke, someone, some of you lazy to read the first chapter may skip it to there, but trust me despite the first chapter is a little bit boring but it's good for you for joking someone because it needs some technique and basis, some of you may suitable with some particular technique because every one of you have different charming, different knowledge or different culture, in general, this book of making a joke I am trying to write it for every one of you, then after reading it, you can apply it to your communication, no matter where you are, which the culture you belong, your mission is picking the most suitable technique and practice it to success, remember that "practice makes perfect" now, I recommend you to sit tight open this book and read carefully for the first technique!

## THE POPULAR METHOD OF JOKE

Over two thousand years ago, Sun Tzu, a Chinese military strategist had written an ancient book "The Art of War" that used this method for the deciding factor of victory, indeed this factor was applied for almost all subjects in the human world not only for war, this book after that was accepted by both eastern countries and western countries, Sun Tzu has written about it in the book: " attack him where he is unprepared, appear where you are not expected", so what Sun Tzu wants to tell us? Let's make it surprised! It's the key to success, one day some curious girls try to ask me:

- *Nicholas, do you have a girlfriend?*

- *Yes, but she came from the other nation*

- *Which nation?*

- *Imagination!*

I don't know why they laughed so hard with the answer although I was answered it in a serious attitude, for making it surprise, the leading element is do not let others know what are you thinking what you will say next, the art of humor is not only keeping your serious face and say the awkward things but also need the formula for it, below there are three basic steps of making something surprising:

Step 1: telling a short tale in serious

Step 2: pulling the tale plot to a climax

Step 3: finishing your tale with an unexpected ending

That simple! This formula will work in case you telling a story with positive meaning or better telling a nonsense story, for some story with negative meaning it will become counteraction worse it may hurt audience feeling also the essence of humor is positive then always be positive if you want to make formulas in this book success

## *Be positive!*

The reason why it(surprise) can make someone laugh because they were felt deceived by you, will you ready to become a cheater, in this case, the cheater that trying to steal someone's heart but to become a cheater you need time to learn to become a cheater, that's a true story!

for doing this formula success you should do it secretly if we say to someone that "hey bro I will joke you" or "I want to tell you a funny story, it's..." their mind (audience) will automatically create a wall for defending your joke, even though you joke them with the best way or best stories you have, trust me, you will fail! So my tip is letting them don't have enough time to prepare for something surprise and never say that "hey! My friend I gonna tell you a funny story" or "I want to tell you a joke" that's a massive failure, on the traveling tour trip, I always tell my customers that " *welcome to the tour in Vietnam in 3 days 2 nights, I'm your tour guide today, my name is Nicholas, from Hanoi to your destination today, it takes 3 hours to travel on this bus, then right now to get started our tour I have a very big gift for you, it is…*

*A bottle of water !"*

( then I gave them water, indeed it's come from my company)

In this introduction of the tour, I have used the form above, three steps by it own was applied in the unexpected ending, it was made people laugh every day, even though I have done it a thousand times for different tour groups, if you pay attention, the climax always staying near to the ending, most sentences were used in the first paragraph was used to describe the place, character, time… that's help the audience imagine more clearly about your tale and understand it, *"in my childhood,I had a grandfather he always said that I should not watch my money that I should watch my health so why I was watching my health someone stole my money, it was my grandfather"* this short tale was told by Jakie Mason, it was recognized as one of the best joke ever in his career because of the surprise, once again the climax is staying near to the ending with a normal way of telling a story, also avoiding of making the audience not tired in listening the storyteller should do it with a short tale and using the concise style as good as possible! Of course, I put this method to the first way because this is the most popular way to joke, someone, everybody in the world can do it with their own story, and if you don't have this technique, my advice is practicing and using it every day, if you fail nothing to lose, your if you succeed you lose nothing, learning to be humor also similar to learning other things, for an example is swimming, everybody at the first time was touch by the coach about some basic techniques such as how to breathe and keeping the air in your lungs, it's the natural balloon or floating of your body and next step is waving your arms gentle in water, everything will be okay, it also

similar to you now when you learning this joke technique for sure, for you in particular, I hope it's work! But if it doesn't work, this method may not suitable for you, then I'd like to tell you a different way on the next page!

## THIS WAY IS BASICALLY

The men go to a bookshop and asking for book

- *hi can you show me where the book name: a happy family?*

- *huh this type of book is science fiction it's located in the first row - the owner said*

- *how about "a model couple" book?*

- *This type of book is martial art belong to Kung Fu book locating in the second row*

- *Well, where is the book "saving for buying a great house"?*

- *This type of book is general delusion, psychotic book row eight*

- *and the book "to be a man of promotion"?*

- *That's a criminal book located in the third row!*

- *and the book " a caring wife "*

- *the fifth row of mythology*

- *How about the most famous book "gentlemen is the pillar of the family"?*

- *Sorry sir! right here, we are not selling fairy tales!*

I believe that some of you may chuckle or smile after reading this story,there's no need to explain too much, the author of this story was used a very popular way of joke "implication", this is the most powerful weapon in communication,in case of using this method for joke , it's can make people laugh immediately then after a long time gone, people were reminded it in their mind and they still feeling funny by themselves, This style mostly using in excellence by Eastern Asia countries because Asian people with the characteristic introvert and the influence from Confucianism, they consider telling something in frankly is a sign of impoliteness then implication is more popular in communication of Eastern Asia people than other continents, to do it successfully my tip is not mentioned directly to the thing you want to say but describe it, it's seem to be complicated but indeed it's really simple, let me give you an example, imagine you're talking about a bull but not mentioned to the name of this animal, let's describe his body, skin, horn, his face, his sound, his habit such as hating the red things, then the audience can recognize it, it's similar to when you tell someone that "I'm vegetarian " then grabbing a pork on the table, eat it immediately, in this case the implication is I'm kidding you!

The advertisement below showing us strongly an implication case:

Okay! Now let's find out the implication of this advertisement,

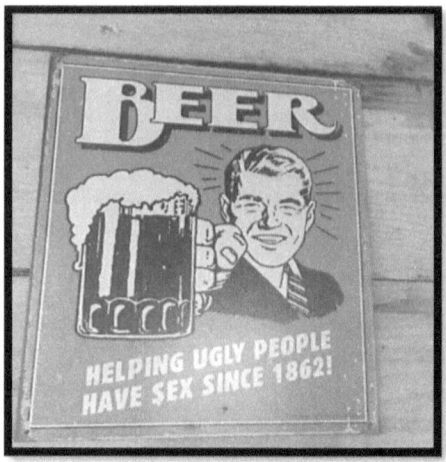

That's simple!
It's come from the research that when people are drunk they will recognize that everybody surrounding them very beautiful, and when people drunk there is a very high capacity of having sex liberally to other people, it is a true story that happens every single day in the whole world and everyone (adult) know clearly about it(a kind of academic joke), otherwise this method similar to a rule in writing, it's "showing, don't tell " when storyteller using this rule he will show the audience the story by describing, this way will make the story more attractive and impressive.
Comparing 2 sentences below:
1. Nicholas is insanely angry


2. Nicholas clenched his teeth, his face turned red, his chin bulged

and sinews rising on his neck

The first sentence (1) "tell" you that Nicholas is angry and the second one (2) "show" you his angry then which one makes you feel impressive?

When you "tell" it's meaning you have summed up or concluded the plot, the audience understands you in a passive way, otherwise when you "show" it's meaning you supplying the detailed information, factors, data… the audience had to link all the things, they will conclude by themself, This period of understanding will make them more exciting, because this method makes the imagination of the audience have to work, for using the implication to become a joke successfully there are 2 basic rules:

- *implying must have the meaning of non-hurting someone's feelings*

Definitely! When you hurting someone's feelings, it's not a joke anymore, it's a tragedy or irritating someone, with the most powerful weapon of communication, you should use it carefully, make love not war is my advice always, implication will become the hallow of kindness and it will become the monster in the hand of a dark heart.

- *Have you been to America?*

- *In my dream!*

Mostly Americans asked me this question and they smile after that answer because I am implied that traveling to America is my dream and I never have been to America for sure, and they keep asking me :

- *what do you want to travel to America?*

- *Tomorrow!*

- *But you need a visa!?*

- *No! Just put me to your suitcase and travel to America!*

Of course! I am Imply an illegal way to them so deeply meaning I'm an illegal man

On two first examples, you will easily recognize that my joke doesn't hurt someone feelings it always succeeds, another day, I travel with my close friend he also an American, we came to a local restaurant and ordering a dish of local chicken for lunch (this kind of chicken is black skin) so when we ordered a chicken, there is only this kind of chicken available in the restaurant and...

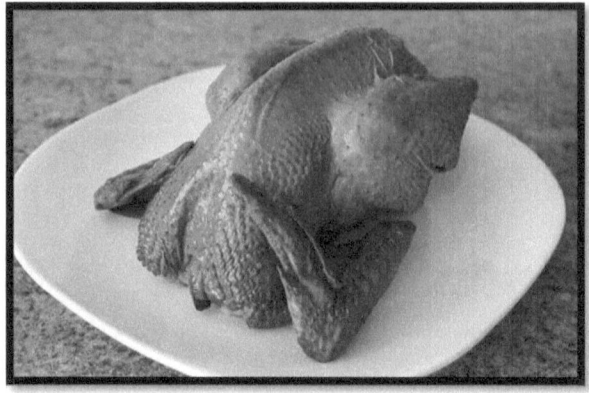

chicken in black

It looks awkward, Maybe they scared of it then on the meal they eat vegetables only, that makes me curious, I ask them:

- *Why don't you eat this!? (I pointed to the chicken plate)*

- *No! I'm scary*

- *Are you racist ???*

This question implies to another subject it's racism in America, that's always hot when someone talking about it, my friend laughs immediately, but after that, I recognized that if he is not my close friend, I will be punched because of this impolite joke, so I recommend you do it only for your close friends, for others it may hurt...

- ***impacting others in a positive way***

As the most powerful weapon of communication implication can make other people feel better by a joke, such as waking up the potential power in someone, defeating their fear or encourage people passing their challenges, if you joke can do it, you are truly saving the whole world, the Irish legend George Bernal Shaw was a dramatist and literary critic, one day he was wandering on the street, suddenly he was crushed by a cycling man, him, after that immediately helped Shaw stand up with apologies repeating on his mouth, Shaw simply flicked off his dust on clothes and said:

*" My friend, you are not lucky! if today you crash me to die, you may become famous in the world !"*

The joke from Shaw implying that when the cycling man crash a famous people to die, his name will be shown in newspapers and of course the whole world will know about it, this joke make the cycling man felt better because it's also implied Shaw is good after the accident because of his joke, the other circumstance happen to Ronald Reagan, one of the greatest presidents in America, One day in 1981 near a hotel in Washington DC the president who was shot in his chest by an assassination attempt,of course! He was brought to the hospital, his wife, the first lady Nancy was come to meet him in an anxious, She was told " *honey, I forgot to duck*" his joke after that became famous on media with implying that he still good, it given American people A hope of recovering political Chaos after the assassination, then he was moved to the surgeon, all doctors, nurses were nervous, They understand that not always they get a chance to do surgeons for a president, maybe they need more experience to do it, especially for their president, In the Surgery room, Reagan still feeling conscious then all people was told by him *"please tell me you are Republican"* immediately the room was filled with laughter, all people feeling better then Reagan has a success, after that he keeps doing his great job as the 40th President of the United States of America

*- showing, don't tell*

*- implying must have the meaning of non-hurting someone's feelings*

*- impacting others in a positive way*

The joke is not express your class but most people in society with high-class usually using it for joke are popular, It is a sign of intelligence and wisdom, when you create a joke with implication style it show a mind with capable of complicated thinking, it will be greater with your warm heart, I consider it as the finest of humor

## A VERY SELDOM WAY

One of the most humorist writers of America is Mark Twain, he was well known as the person was born and died in the same year that Halley's Comet flew by the earth, he was commented: " *I came in with Halley's comet in 1835, it is coming again Next year and I expected to go out with it, it will be the greatest disappointment of my life if I don't go out with Halley's comet, The Almighty has said, no doubt: wow here are these two unaccountable Freak, they came in together, they must go out together"*

His wish after that definitely come true! Mark Twain who was famous for so many funny speeches or commentary, Does his comment above make you chuckle? even though his wish come true or not, we cannot deny the truth that he is a funny person, an important person of US literature, as a humorous writer, Mark Twain has so many techniques in-joke, At the last his comment, his technique is the comparison and even though people said that:

"all comparison all lame" yes, if you want to do this technique injoke successfully, let's make it lame, to do this technique becomes a joke there are two basic ways:

- contrast comparison

- Similar comparison

**contrast comparison**

To make it lame in this comparison is not hard, for the first case of this, we will learn Mark Twain once again, he is also interested in politic when he was alive, One day he disagreed with an Act that was approved by Congress then he posted an article on newspaper with the title: "*half of the congressional staff are bastard*" after publishing, So many phone calls came to him as offenses and protests, congressional staff also angry and disagree about it, they tried to force Mark Twain to disclaim it, the pressure is getting higher and higher, it's forced Mark Twain have to disclaim his article, finally he had to publish a disclaimer, it said that: "*sorry I was wrong! about congressional staff, the haft of them are not bastard*"

Okay, now let's see how Mark Twain joke, exactly it is a satirical implication

| haft of congressional staff are bastards | haft of congressional staff are not bastards |

That's contrast, same same but different in one sentence that changed his disclaiming become a trick and further it is a joke

And a comedian was said that: "*There are only two categories on the diving there's a grand champion and stuff on a rock*" The same way also, you can recognize how massive distance from grand champion to the stuff remaining on the rock, we can see it rely on the situation or circumstance and from them the speaker could find out the opposite thing of it, to make it become a success, it should be practiced to become a habit, a habit that you will use it skillfully in communication, anyway Practice makes perfect, through these examples above we saw that all them having the same point in comparison it's a pair of comparison always have a large distance with each other, and the comparison seems to be trying stressed on that, right now so many of you may think well it is so easy to create a joke with this way, I say not yet! it is not enough to make

someone chuckles when you are lacking one more important element, without it the comparison becomes trivial comparison such as the pair of water- fire, black-white, bad smell-good smell…etc, I mean it needs to touch to the imagination of the audience, in this case, my advice is the more lively of comparison you make the better joke you do, it is said that in the time of the cold war between the United States of America and the Soviet Union, President Ronald Reagan in the convention of the white house, after a long time of discussion and facing many questions about the war, he replied to reporters: "here is my strategy on Cold War: We win, they lose" this speech after that became famous because of its funny meaning, However, contrast comparison not always work good, it depends on how you say it, how the distance of the opposition in comparing with each other, what you talking about make audience imagination work or not, in conclusion, the rules of success in-joke in contrast comparison are:

- *Making the opposition as far as possible*

- *Let's audience imagination work*

**Similar comparison**

It seems to be awkward to talk about it, then you may think that if they are similar with each other, there's nothing else to compare, that's the paradox but it's paradox creates the funny things, a US standup comedian was said that: *"babies are like poems, They are beautiful to their creator, but to other people, they are silly and they are irritating"* let guests the reaction of the audience in his show, they laugh!

The technique to do this kind of joke is comparing the similar point of two different things, that's sound stupid, but this is the key of success in a similar comparison, one day I was chuckled when my friend described me a girl and her beauty, he said: *"From far away I saw her already, she is beautiful with eyes of a Husky dog!"*

From the first and second example above, we see that The speaker has used the same technique

Example 1:

- Difference: babies and poem are different

- Similar points: they are beautiful To their creators, but to other people, they are silly and they are irritating

And example 2:

- Difference: a human girl and a Husky dog

- Similar point: their eyes

With this formula, we can joke anybody in the world successfully, but to make it more effective we should ensure the rule:

## Let audience imagination work

By success similar comparison another thing we need after learning the above formula is meaning, the comparison should have it own meaning or imply something in particular, if you make it no sense, you fail! From the example above we have seen the meaning of it :

- Example 1: babies make other people annoyed ( implication)

- Example 2: she has such beautiful eyes (implication)

And this is an example of a failed joke:

# ART OF HUMOR

- *"Jakie Chan is Asian, Rowan Atkinson is English but both of them are handsome"*

- *"Michael Jackson is men, Lady Gaga is women but both of them sing very well"*

That's a nonsense example because nothing lively from that and audience imagination not work, on the contrary, some commentaries below you may see it interesting in every subject:

- Politics: he is Donal Trump of England ( imply Borish Johnson)

- Sport: He is a Messi of Asia (depend on the country you're staying )

- Physics: -When a man sits with a pretty girl for two hours it seems to be like a minute but when you sit on a hot stove for a minute you might think it's two hours, it's relativity -Albert Einstein-

- Movie: some people can read War and Peace and come away thinking it's a simple adventure story, others can read On a chewing gum wrapper and unlock the secret of the universe - Lex Luthor (superman - 1978)

- It is a funny joke of Cold War- history: "An American explain to a Russian that the United States is a truly free country Because he can stand in front of the White House and shout "to hell with Ronal Reagan", Russian say that is nonsense because he can easily stand in Red Square and shout "to hell with Ronal Reagan"

- Sex: A family is at the dinner table. The son asks the father, "Dad, how many kinds of boobs are there?" The father, surprised, answers, "Well, son, a woman goes through three phases. In her 20s, a woman's breasts are like melons, round, and firm. In her 30s and 40s, they are like pears, still nice, hanging a bit. After 50, they are like onions." "Onions?" the son asks. "Yes. You see them and they make you cry." This infuriated his wife and daughter. The daughter asks, "Mom, how many different kinds of willies are there?" The mother smiles and says, "Well, dear, a man goes through three phases also. In his 20s, his willy is like an oak tree, mighty and hard. In his 30s and 40s, it's like a birch, flexible but reliable. After his 50s, it's like a Christmas tree." "A Christmas tree?" the daughter asks. "Yes, dead from the root up and the balls are just for decoration."[1]

Hopefully, with the formula and example above, you can choose your style and do it with successfully.

---

[1] source: Laugh Factory

## THE DIRTY WAY

From a long time ago, sexual and joke have been connected with each other as one of the most ancient ways to make someone laugh,sex the need is necessary as food or drinking,i am sure that lacking of this human may become crazy along history of mankind, when someone growing adult the need of sex was programmed in their brain already, i name it as the mind of sex,it's always waiting for rising when it have a chance or when it have enough condition, so it is not so hard to understand why this subject alway make the imagination of so many people work hard,so it doesn't hard to understand when something sexual appear in joke with the last purpose is raising the mind of sex in everybody,This style commonly using by western countries,especially in America because of the development of sexual revolution in 1960s, with the freedom of speech for a long time it had created the open mind for people in every fields, especially for making a joke, then to day on media, it is not so hard to find a sexual joke but how to do it effectively, for some people it's still a big question!

by both directly way and indirectly way this is also the best way to impress human brain in common joke, but sometimes the rude person use it in the wrong way then it's may make the other feeling allergy, So this way of making a joke was considered as the dirty way with so many bad rumors or scandals, that is the reason why I name it as the dirty way of a joke, and this book was written for improving the way people using this hallow

**Indirectly way**

The dirty way there are two basic ways of it, indirectly and directly! For more effectively to use it in public or for the other people do not know you very well in communication, I recommend you (all the people reading this book) to use the first way of it as the indirectly way, the technique to perform it is the implication, the best way to impress the human brain, it also forces imagination work in our brain, the example below there will show us more clearly " *Why did I get divorced? Well, last week was my birthday, my wife didn't wish me a happy birthday. my parents forgot and so did my kids. I went to work and even my colleagues didn't wish me a happy birthday. As I entered my office, my secretary said, "Happy birthday, boss!" I felt so special. She asked me out for lunch. After lunch, she invited me to her apartment. We went there and she said, "Do you mind if I go into the bedroom for a minute?" "Okay," I said. She came out 5 minutes later with a birthday cake, my wife, my parents, my kids, my friends, & my colleagues all yelling, "SURPRISE!!!" while I was waiting on the sofa... naked*[2]"

It's nothing rude with the example above, the author doesn't mention anything sexual, the only thing that makes our imagination work

---

[2] source: Laugh Factory

it's the word "naked", keep the audience imagination working is not hard, the thing you need only drawing some basic brush strokes then the audience will see the whole picture, from a long time ago something sexual or dirty can make human imagination work hardly such as boobs, breast, buttock, shit, pole dancing... or something like that was used for this kind of joke, as long as you don't mention it by directly way, audience imagination will work, in the Rush Hour series movie, Chris Tucker was mocked his girlfriend by the question *"Hey girl! What's the color of the pantie you wear?"* That isn't rude of this mocking but the audience brain has work to imagine the girl's pantie color, That's why people laugh so hard in this case.

In my experience traveling I have a chance to talk with so many young tourists and using this technique to test it in reality, luckily this kind of joke work really effectively, when we have kayaking on Halong bay with each other, I told them about the legend of the bay, the floating village, fish farming, oyster farming, the daily life of local people such as singing karaoke on the boat with happy water(I mean rice wine) and especially the massive power of the oysters that they(young tourists) ate last night, with a solemn face as a president of the bay, I said:

- me: *oyster! It's expensive right here because it has so much nutrition and it's very good for the gentleman. Do you know why?*

- Tourists: *why???*

- Me: *because if one man eats so many oysters he is very strong on the bed...and also if you eat about 5 to 10 oysters at night, you will destroy your girlfriend!*

- Tourists: *(laughing)*

- Me: *so! If you haven't tried it last night, I recommend you to kayak around here, buy some! Go home and eat a little bit, I think your girlfriend will not disappointed!*

- Tourists:(laugh one more time)

I consider that It's the most successfully joke on the tour ever because I did it a thousand times for different tour groups each journey, then I thought I have found out the formula of a joke, because I believe that everybody has a dirty mind inside them, some of them sometimes try to hide it, and your mission in this joke is wake it up and let it have breakfast, then following the basic rules below to have a successful joke from chuckle:

- *avoiding mention to sexual by directly way*

- *Touching the audience imagination by implication of sexual or disgusting things*

Another example showing that dirty joke work effectively with strongly impacting human brain it refer to the incident was happened in the event FiFa European Football Championship 2016 with the weird behavior of Germany manager Joachim Low when he watching his team on field such as picking nasal mucus then putting it in his mouth,scratching the armpit and checked if it smell good or not,scratching his arse and sniffing it after, all the sceneries were filmed and repeated many times on television that make people in the world cannot stop laughing with his disgusting action although Joachim Low did not do anything wrong and I recommend you stop read this page in a moment to search it on google with keywords "Joachim low disgusting moments" to understand more about what am I trying to tell you, moreover in cinema Rowan Atkinson is the comedian know this technique and apply it in reality very well ,about 70 percent of filming in toilet becoming success with mr Bean, in that some sceneries imply dirty in toilet were favorited by audience,and thank to the toilet, it made his nickname "the man who loves toilet"

There are some cases below that people add it to conversation for a joke by implying in popularity :

- my banana - my penis

- My cucumber - also my penis

- Her Pomellos - her boobs

- Pole dancing sexy - seduce someone by sexual way

# ART OF HUMOR

- Naked - they will do something funny in the future

- This can make you stronger on the bed - something can buff gentleman power midnight

- Practicing exercise on the bed - making love

- Shallow swimming(uncommon way) - also making love

- Made in Paris, born in Denmark- let do honeymoon in Paris

- There is no happy ending tonight - nothings funny tonight

- Number 69 - Number 69

**Directly way**

This type of joke, the main purpose is shocking audience by mentioning directly to sexual or the sensitive part of the human body, The speaker also mention or describe the disgusting things, disgusting things in this case what I mean is something dirty but not horrible because describe the horrible things such as a bloody accident is not a joke it makes audience scary and running far away you, so remember describing disgusting things only, then it will be more comfortable to do this type to your close friend or generous audience, directly way also using as the strongest way of emotional expression in communication, Such as warning your friend do not kid to someone:

- *"he's very serious, don't fuck with him"*

Or making a complaint:

- *oh shit! I never saw anybody stupid like him*

Of course we should be conscious to realize which complaint is for fun which is in seriousness, You also expressed disappointment by saying: oh shit, but if you and your buddy see a big poop floating on your pool, and you still saying oh shit! : it will turn into a funny joke!

as an author I recognize the direct way of the joke is not impolite it is only impolite when the speaker uses it in wrong time also the wrong audience, my advice is limit to use it as few as possible because it is a double-edged sword, it protects you also possible to kill you for sure, however I still set it there because I'm the author of this book and my responsibility is guiding to use this sword and make sure you are not hurt yourself.

The direct way of this joke also use for swearing, when you and other people suffering a difficult situation then the general feeling is need something to clear stressful far away, this type of joke will work effectively in this case:

"*Oh shit! What a fucking traffic jam*" or more creative: "*what a mother fucking stuck traffic*" by mentioning directly to sexual such as boobs, buttock, vaginal, dick, penis, some disgusting things...that joke normally successfully because of shocking audience imagination but not enough for making audience imagination work, The key of every successful joke is making the imagination work, as long as the imagination work harder the joke is better, so what we have to do to make audience imagination work? You will find it out easily by reading a sexual tale below:

A boy says to a girl, "*So, sex at my place?*" "*Yeah!*" "*Okay, but I sleep in a bunk bed with my younger brother, and he thinks we're making sandwiches, so we have to have a code. Cheese means faster and tomato means harder, okay?*" *Later on the girl is yelling,* "*Cheese cheese, tomato tomato!*" *The younger brother says, "Stop making sandwiches! You're getting mayo all over my bed!"* [3]

I believe that your imagination may work very well in this tale, especially the first time you read this tale, Although it wasn't described in detail, it still making us feel something really disgusting or stinking right here(mayo from tomato and cheese) in this case the author has described it in detail by adding the disgusting things(red liquid on the bed from tomato and cheese) to joke, imagination the liquid from food remaining on a white bed it makes the audience have a slimy feeling this is exactly intention that author harboring,i am sure this image is unacceptable for some of you, but anyway the only thing they want is forcing your imagination has to work, work hard!

---

[3] source: Laugh Factory

In particularly to do this type of joke successfully for sure, you should be a solemn person or pretending to become a solemn person, then cursing will break your image in audience eyes, this method also were used by some stand up comedians such as Kevin Hart, Russle Peter the audience was surprised with broken image is the key to success in this type of joke, Kevin Hart have used it in the show My first time cursing, in the show Kevin was described as a cute kid but later The audiences were shocked with his cursing, it is the period of changing from a cute boy to a little bastard, that's breaking image ,his mother also described as a respectful mommy, solemn lady until she tries to tell her son saying cursed words to his teacher because of her disagree after she received a complaint note about her son from school : *"tell her to mind her damn business, before I go down there and beat her ass "and when Kevin want to confirm it once again, she continued "Kevin, if I tell you once again I will smash your shit out!"*, Kevin after that went to school and tell his teacher exactly what *he was told by his respectful mother: "my mom told me to tell you to mind your mother fucking business bitch! Little stupid bitch! Little dump teacher bitch...long tits and no nipple bitch!"*

Audience were laughed out loud with these moments, not only shocking but also breaking image of all characters, indeed no mom teach her son say cursed word and also no kid dare to cursing to teacher,the show ended with the suspended to Kevin, poor him,but audience need it to make the show drama, once again the shocking technique bring a high effectively in joke when audience's emotion step by step controlled by Kevin's joke, it not only a joke but also an art of controlling other people emotion, in my tour guide career sometime in some circumstances i have to use it as unavoidable answer when one day, i travelled with a family(4 tourists) from Switzerland and they have a dad really love vietnamese pomelo,you know this kind of tropical fruit may lead to undefendable consequence in stomach if you eat it in vietnam, at that day after lunch they tried to persuaded me to eat pomelo with each other, a massive pomelo, of course i refused and their dad an old man 60 years old trying to find out the reason why?

- Tourist: *why don't you eat some, are you afraid of something poison in it?*

- Me: *no sir, it's safe!*

- Tourist: *tell me why?*

- Me: *because eating pomelo may make us lose control in making*

*fart on the bus*

It immediately makes all family laugh out loud and finally all of us have to open the window on the bus all time!

so after all the direct way of joke will succeed if we ensure the basic rules:

- *Shocking audience by sexual or cursing*

- *Describing sexual or disgusting things in detail (slimy, stinking…)*

- *Pretending to be a solemn person for doing this joke*

There are some funny joke was used in common (indicating for a close friend, generous person only)

- *I am helping you bitch!* ( in case of buddy misunderstand you)

- *Lift your ass and do it!* (in case of someone lazy)

- *I will beat your ass* (You disagree with someone)

- *I am gonna kick your ass* (when playing a game with a buddy)

- *He's having a breast of 16-year-old girl* (his boobs are big)

- *You are a crazy bitch* (be a serious buddy)

- *I don't like that shit* ( I really don't like it, buddy)

- *I need some nipples for tonight* (i need sex)

- *Are you finding a new girl with bigger boobs* (are you changing your girlfriend buddy)

- *It's the biggest pomelo I have seen before* (when you tell a friend about a special girl)

- *Go home bitch! you are drunk*(implying someone doing something crazy)

- *Stupid ass*( Your buddy need to teach his ass some lesson)

- *I have a back pocket as a bitch*( when you don't have a good Allie

Above are some examples of cursing in-joke, for ending the part of a dirty joke, we will finish with a tale that ensures 3 basic rules:

"*A mother is in the kitchen making dinner for her family when her daughter walks in. "Mother, where do babies come from?" The mother thinks for a few seconds and says, "Well dear, Mommy and Daddy fall in love and get married. One night they go into their bedroom, they kiss and hug, and have sex." The daughter looks puzzled so the mother continues, "That means the daddy puts his penis in the mommy's vagina. That's how you get a baby, honey." The child seems to comprehend. "Oh, I see, but the other night when I came into your room you had daddy's penis in your mouth. What do you get when you do that?" "Jewelry, my dear. Jewelry."* [4]

---

[4] source: *Laugh factory*

## A VERY HOT WAY

Human psychology always tending being attracted by something famous or becoming famous, that's Human! And something famous also interesting things by itself, that is the reason why I say the famous is interesting because I haven't seen anything famous is boring, so when something or someone famous it had to be interesting, spending a minute to think about it then you will recognize that it right, now you may wonder that we are talking about joke, so what the relationship between the famous and joke? Definitely, it's a tight relationship, the key of this joke are interesting things, This kind of joke commonly make other people chuckle because it's technique is not so strong to impress other people or shock them to laugh as implication or dirty joke absolutely not! this kind of joke work effectively if you use it in public, its technique is gentle but not mild

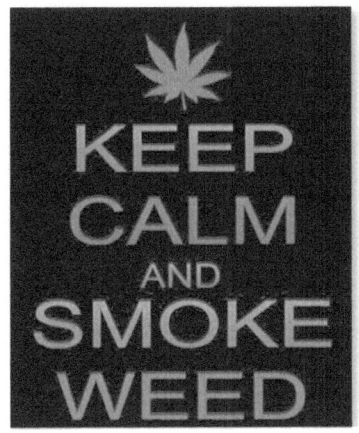

The poster was used to print on t-shirt following a traditional famous motivational poster produced by the British government in 1939 in preparation for World War II and the original of it is:

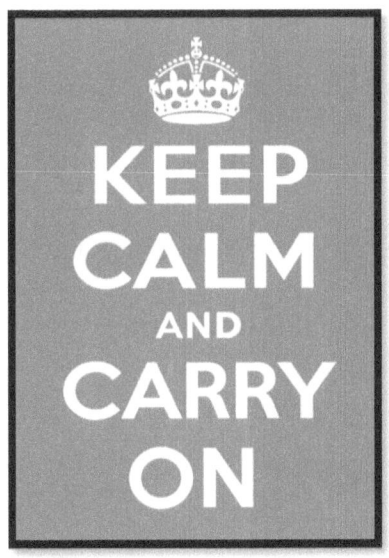

Nowadays, it's still hot speech in the world with so many more creative speech using the structure "keep calm and..." to joke the other people, in my experience I have used it with tourists on the bus when I try to let them learn Vietnamese in my own way, Because Vietnamese is hard to learn, then before starting to teach them this language, I have to tell them that you should "keep calm and learn Vietnamese" this make them laugh then it makes me wonder why people easy to laugh with it,it make me realize something magic from this form, then it become another way to joke others from that moment, The same formula to make this joke successfully Is using famous speech from famous people, The trending speech or trending banner,slogans from many companies in the world with their own advertisement, when you get it and you created by your own way to joke others is not enough, It's need another factor knowledge audience, you might say some trending speech by your own way very funny, but it will be nothing if the audience don't know that famous trending speech,then the basic rule of this kind of joke is:

- ***using a famous or trending speech in your own way***

- ***The audience has to know the famous or trending speech that you are talking about***

For doing joke success from a chuckle, The more famous a speech you use The more success you have, and when you fail in trying to joke, someone, it will not make you feel embarrassed as the other joke, it's the advantage of this joke, easier than ever and the only thing you do is choosing the most suitable time to say it, for this kind of joke the practical joker don't need to be talkative for expressing themselves as a funny person their mission is to keep listening to their friend and say it in a suitable time, it similar to a weaker boxer against an opponent on the arena, his opponent too strong and he has to keep defending all the time, the remaining mission is finding opponent mistake and throw the decided punch to knock-out him.

For the people don't have the capability of humor or saying something funny, this kind of joke is the easiest for practicing, if you know someone like that, let's give them this book and show them this page I hope it will not make them disappointed, so now if you are confident with all the things you have learned, just do it!

Just do it! The famous slogan of Nike is my favorite speech in Tour Guide job, it encourages people to do something faster when they are in hesitation, one day on the bay near to Cat Ba island, we did cliff jumping from the top of 15 meters high, some people have decided to do that in the beginning of the tour, the group were told that "if you decided to do that, you have to do that because when you climb up to the cliff in the middle of the bay the boat carrying us now will leave us immediately, then no way back, you have to jump off the cliff then swim back to the boat, I led a group of 9 people (7 mens and 2 girls), the cliff jumping is smoothly until an American girl she is the last person, She was really scary and nearly cry, the group and me have used so many ways to force her to jump but fail, including singing US National anthem or reading Abraham Lincoln Gettybug speech…., later I told her a tip *" do not looking down to the water keep looking the horizon,close your eyes and jump! just do it !!"* The group swimming in water also yelled *"just do it"* with a laugh and applause, she (the last girl staying on a cliff) also laugh and jump after that, we took 30 minutes to do it with fear, tears, bravery, US national anthem, political speech, Nike banner, and thank God finally it success, although some people yell: finally ! as soon as she jumped!

The cliff jumping after that was banned by the government because somebody was hurt themselves with doing the wrong technique in jumping, I don't have any chance to do cliff jumping anymore but the banner just do it has become my slogan to encourage other people or remind them to do something, for you to people is reading this book also use my slogan for a joke, you can practice it from now, just do it!

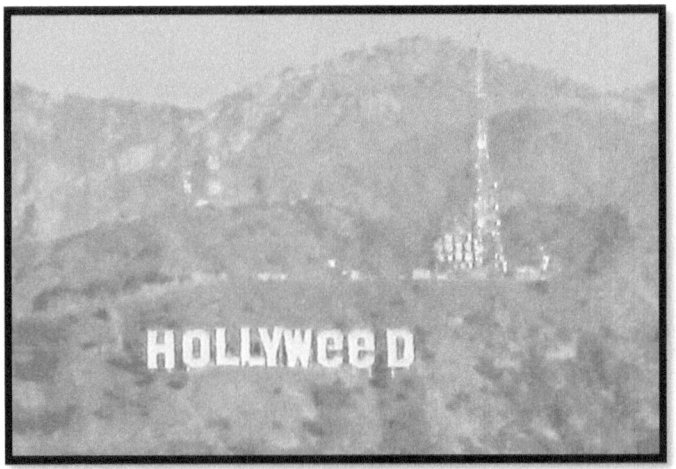

This image definitely a joke?, no! that's real, the famous icon of world movie capital was altered by a man who loves weed, with the hopes of inspiring legislators in California to legalize cannabis in

2017, he is may disappoint because California citizens just consider it as a prank, they laugh when someone talks about it except policemen, another striking demonstration that using the famous banner or trending speech then creative in their own way for joke successfully, this prank proven that when the basic rules were ensured, it works effectively for a joke, if you need some trending speech to learn for a joke, below there are some famous sentences were used in popular:

- *keep calm and carry-on*

- *We need you*

- *It's gonna be legendary*

- *Challenge accepted*

- *Change do it*

- *Never say never*

- *Mission impossible*

- *It's undefendable*

- *It's Undefeatable*

- *I want it that way*

- *You are apple of my eyes*

- *Make America great again*

One of the best sceneries of Rush hour 2 refer to Chris Tucker, he was played as a police, James Carter (black American) have tried to join a table in a casino, but the crew considers him as a trouble because of his talkative, James after that blame them " *are you racist!*" A squad of guards was surrounding him because of crew order, they want kick him out, but the situation was changed, James has a forceful speech to the public *"I have a dream that white people and black people and even Chinese people can gamble together without getting different chips"* The crowd surrounding him was blown with applause, racists are lost, The scenery end with his speech *"in the spirit of brotherhood let's play crab man!! come on! come on!"*, The scenery after that was favorited by the audience in the world because of its drama, slogan "I have a Dream" before that was famous for public speech that was delivered by American civil rights activist Martin Luther King Jr, in the speech he called for civil and economic rights and an end to racism in the United States of America, there is only one different thing between them, it's Martin Luther King's speech use it to struggle for civil rights and Chris Tucker use it to struggle for gambling, the parody of James Carter(Chris Tucker) was become famous because it's a mini version of King's speech and the coincidence is both of them are black Americans, this slogan rise the imagination of the audience, that's why people find it funny (one of the basic rules in humor), anyway despite a different culture, language or nation, this kind of joke can become a success as soon as you are following the basic rules:

- *using a famous or trending speech by yourself own way*

- *The audience has to know the famous or trending speech that you are talking about*

## A VERY HARD WAY

Now you are reading this part, a question may emanating from your mind "are you serious, how can I do it when you see that way hard?" My answer is "yeah, I'm definitely serious now" Because each of you are different people with different abilities, so your mission after reading this book is picking a style of joke that suitable your ability,this kind of joke I will show you may be hard for some people,however, it may be easy for some body that having character suitable with it, honestly, I still feeling this kind of joke is hard,i have found out this kind of joke one day, in a New Year's party of my friend company, both of staff and bosses are staying together in our group, in my friend group there is a bald guy he has no hair because of alopecia, we were enjoying the party with happy-water(rice wine), then the waiter brought a small tray of happy water cup come to us, then he gave it one by one to all people,suddenly the waiter dropped a cup of happy-water on the head of bald guy, the party has become quite, all people look to the waiter in silent and stunned, the bald guy whom is the victim of this incident turned himself back to the water with a serious face:

"hey guy! You think this method can treat my alopecia??"-The bald guy asked, the party was blown with laugh and applause the situation was changed 180 degrees, the bald guy also laugh with the crew for proving this incident doesn't matter to him, I recognize that he is a generous and optimistic person, who cannot be defeated in any situation, and if I were him, I may not laugh after that, the situation may become worse with saying some cursed words, so to do this joke successfully you should be a calm or patient man in any situation, it is also an ability of gentleman, this kind of joke is a self-deprecating joke, in that the speaker will make a joke about himself his shortcoming or his culture, I recognize this kind of joke is hard because not everyone has the capacity of realizing their shortcomings, it's very hard to accept by yourself that oh I'm so stupid in this case, well I'm fat, I'm ugly, I'm short, I'm old... so to accept it you have to be a confident person, do you have any shortcomings? If you are perfect maybe this kind of joke is not for you, then I recommend you to fold it and go to the next page, please don't throw it away, keep calm and learn the humor

**What is your shortcoming?**

Now we recognize that the first basic rule is realizing your shortcomings, we will learn the next rule with Abraham Lincoln one of the greatest presidents of the United States of America, this circumstance happened before he became president, in the anecdote was told that Lincoln, one day, while he was riding a horse through the woods, he was described as "features the lady could not call handsome" he met a woman on horseback. He waited for her to pass, but she stopped in turn and said:

- *"Well, for land sake, you are the homeliest man I ever saw."*

- *"Yes madam . . . but I can't help it,"* he replied.

- *"No, I suppose not,"* said the lady, *"but you might stay at home."*

- *"Madam, it is the only thing that I cannot do"* Lincoln said

In this case, Their first reaction was settled, but for other, people may get angry and retaliate this impolite woman by trying to find out some of her shortcomings to insult her, but Lincoln wasn't doing that, he changed his shortcoming become a joke "I can not help that" also implied that he can't improve his appearance, he may absolutely surrender in trying to be handsome, also showing the personal shortcoming in the optimist way is a sign of high EQ person

# ART OF HUMOR

## *showing the shortcoming in a positive way*

This second basic rule seems to be complicated to understand because it relies on the situation in particular, my tip is finding out the advantage of your shortcomings by asking yourself some questions such as what is the benefit of your shortcoming? what you can do with your shortcoming? as if you are an ugly girl you can tell your friend that *"I don't need to make up this Halloween"* or *"if I am walk on the street everybody may feel that today is Halloween"* if you are too short let say " when someone is talking to me they have to talk with their head bowed down" or relying on Napoleon Bonaparte's quote "The greatness of a man is not measured from his feet to his head, but from his head to sky" in conclusion you need to do it by optimistic way, maybe the person most excellent in this kind of joke is Socrates( 469-399 BC) a classical Greek philosopher, it said that he has a wife name Xanthippe, She was remembered as a shrew a scolding wife, it was said that one day Xanthippe yelled at her husband then she threw a bowl of slops on his head,this incident was happened in front of Socrates students,all students seem to be annoyed with that, but Socrates just smile and said *"Did i not say that Xanthippe's thunder would end in rain"* that made his students laugh out loud, then he keep teaching students the new lesson, with this joke,Socrates was proved himself as a gentleman, generous person with strong spirit, I'm not sure some of you reading this page can keep calm with a wife like Xanthippe or not

Once when Socrates invited his friend for lunch in his family for some reasons, Xanthippe came up to them in a rage and scolded them roundly, finally upsetting the lunch table, Socrates crew deeply offended got up and was about to leave, but Socrates just said *"as if we were eating here and the hen fly in for trick"* this made crew laugh with each other they move to another place for lunch, since that time when someone complaining or asking him about his wife,

Socrates just answered: "*by all means, marry, if you get a good wife you will be happy if you get a bad one, you will be a philosopher*" this quote later become legendary for the next generation and for men who owned the bad wife but cannot change! Through this joke Socrates was changed his shortcoming become great, this joke doesn't hurt someone, it was considered as the finest of humor for whom know themselves well, this joke also protects you from criticizing, so many books were written about this joke, some of them said that: "*when you doing this joke it similar to you slapping yourself to expect forgiveness when you did something wrong to your friend*" that's right, how can someone criticize you, when you criticize yourself already, that is the art of joke, from the beginning I said it as a difficult way, because some of you may not know yourself very well if you know yourself well, your self-deprecating joke will become a success when you follow 2 basic rules:

- *realizing and accepting your shortcomings*

- *Showing your shortcoming in a creative and positive way*

What is your shortcoming? What your shortcomings can be used for? Let sit down, keep calm and think about it carefully because sometimes in some circumstances you may have to use it to change your difficult situation or make you become an attractive person, good luck!

## A VERY CHARMING WAY

when is the last time you received a compliment from someone that said "wow! you are so charming!"? yesterday? the day after yesterday? Last week or so many years ago? well if the answer is so many years ago please don't be upset because this question implies the charm of your appearance, The Charming I am talking to you start from inside of you, inside your mind and especially your facial muscles, now, imagine that there are 2 guys stay in 2 different rooms, all of them start for singing, the first guy will sing with micro the song Baby shark with a face of non-expression

The second guy also sing with micro the same song

with an expressive face, the song will be performed in the mood of lovely men, which guy do you prefer? Of course,commonly the second guy will be more preferred than the last one,facial expression always make other people feeling impress in conversation (I recommend to read a book name : definitive book of body language - Allan and Barbara Pease to know more details) It's belong to non-verbal communication,so many people who striking in this field and still famous for this in the world ,which character below you know most: Mr Bean-Rowan attkitson,Achmed (dead terrorist puppet), Donal Trump(Sometime he's not funny but his face betrayed him), Charlie Chaplin this people or character success in their career at least thank to facial expressions, above people having a flexible expressive face and when they talk or performing something, it impressed the human brain,it is a case of humor, we can see the basic thing they do is expressive magnification,This is the reason why today on social network such as Facebook or Tweeter there are so many funny comments by images got much of laugh reaction, most of them are expressing emotion about topic in magnification, and if you have a good facial muscle with flexible expression, congratulations! you have good potential to do this kind of joke, imagination your face is an amplifier your emotion is melody of the song, your facial mission is magnifying it double or triple time, there are 9 fundamentals emotions: Love, pride, sorrow, astonishment, sarcasm, fear, disgust, fury and peace then the more facial expression you have the more successful joke you do, I will perform it here:

Love —> extreme lovely

Pride—> pridefully

Sorrow—>extreme sorrow

Fear——> really fear

Astonishment——> really Astonishment

Sarcasm—> extreme sarcasm

Disgust——> extreme Disgust

Peace——>super calm

You will be charming in case of expressing above emotion for a joke, but using in the solemn situation is not recommended, there is a case of joke that applied this form have performed successfully is in a contest name American got talent the candidate name Andy Rowell from Chicago have to conquer examiners and audience with karaoke singing only one word "tequila" on the stage with a super calm face, simply but the show appreciated with laugh and applause, especially he kept his super calm face in any situation.

if you pay attention in the series of Harry Potter movie the character Ron Weasly (played by Rubert Grint) in the episode of the secret chamber, audience cannot forget the funny expression of Ron when he scared in the cave of spiders (actually Rubert Grint really afraid of spiders) his capable of playing in Ron Weasly after that was nominated for so many prizes in his career as a successful actor thank to his flexible facial expression, Donald Trump before elected to become the 45th president of the USA, he was a television personality so the capable of facial expression was shaped him as unpredictable person(actor skill), this skill after that was shown in position of US president, although his speech really solemn but the audiences still feeling something funny emanate from him, in any speech or any situation his facial expression always funny even though his speech talking to a serious problem such as the death of Islamic State leader or China trade war,indeed we can't stop laughing with his sense of humor,the same case is Rowan Atkinson the man was played as mr Bean and famous for this character, do you feel mr Bean Image in your mind when you reading this sentence! Him (Rowan Atkinson) an icon of awkward men, the face with awkward expression is the cause of bullying from his classmates, his expressive face in every episode of Mr. bean make the audience cannot stop laughing, this case was proven that nonverbal having a massive power in a funny joke,it's also true to the same circumstance but not a real man, i'm mentioning to Achmed (dead terrorist puppet) that played by a ventriloquist Jeff Dunham, that appeared on the Internet as sensation because of his face, The show talked about how he dead as a suicide bomber especially the flexible face with impress expression and simply motion of Achmed facial parts such as rising eyebrows,opening mouth for yelling,threatening in glower, if you turn on YouTube and watch him on Internet I am sure that you will learn something interesting from him,If you have a good capable of facial expression,I recommend this kind of joke for you, on the contrary you don't have it, I still having other kind of joke to show you in the next page of this book,the basic rule of this joke will finish this first charming way:

- ***facial expressive magnification plays a supplementary role to joke***

The next charming way of joke directed us to an exercise, you are reading this book for learning joke in another special process, let read the sentence below with different mood or tone of voice, The first practice time, the require is reading the sentence below as an empty voice:

- *it's gonna be legendary*

The second time let try it different with an excited voice:

- *It's gonna be...legendary!!*

It's the exactly way how Barney Stinson say it in the film series How I met your mother, this speech after that was become famous in the world because of its expression, through exercise we can see the different shades of sentences above *"it's gonna be legendary"* at first it seem to be doesn't make sense, nothing funny from it, but if we say it by the second way everything were changed,the key of it is the capable of expression (tone of voice), it impressed directly to our brain and leading us to chuckle,Kevin Hart a famous stand up comedian of Hollywood,he was well known as telling common stories in the common life,such as first time cursing,Kevin Hart in the club,Uncle Richard...for other people perform those tales it doesn't make sense but through Kevin Hart performing,you will feel it funny,especially his tone of voice in emotional expression is the stressed on his tales because the tales he told the audience are his experiences,so the emotion still saving in him then it emanate from when he performed it to audience, another comedian having the same style, Chris Tucker the man with high accent always makes the audience laugh even though he haven't start his tale, once again the effect of expressive magnification play an important role in joke, basically the thing they just do is changing from natural voice to magnifical expressive voice, once again the form of expression prove it's effectively:

Love —> extreme lovely

Pride—> pridefully

Sorrow—>extreme sorrow

Fear——> really fear

Astonishment—-> really Astonishment

Sarcasm—> extreme sarcasm

Disgust——> extreme Disgust

Peace——>super calm

NICHOLAS SANTA CLORE

For trying this kind of joke, the simple process is reminding one of your stories in the past, experience and practice to tell it with your emotional, magnifying your expression as the way of comedian or actor, actress does, hopefully, it will work good with you and it's suitable for your style, both facial expression and voiced expression, good luck!

## A VERY COMPLICATED WAY

I call this as a complicated way because this kind of joke including many tips to do, But in final, all the tips leading to only one subject: make it lame, how to tell a lame story for a joke, how to joke other people by making a lame speech?, in conclusion, this is a complex way of a lame joke, then I will show you one by one from simplest to most complicated.

I'm writing this book now, this moment is december 2019, the world is facing to so many problems,but the most trending news I'm hearing right now come from America, The scandal of US president Donald Trump in Ukraine diplomacy lead to his impeachment, this incident was divided American people, some of them support Trump impeachment, on the contrary some of them are against it, on the BBC newspaper I have read an article from Jonathan Turley (BBC co-worker) commentary about it,that using a technique of this joke,in general Jonathan said this impeachment should not be did,because it may push America to chaos with the next president in the future whom have the same incidence,then he continue talking about Americans reaction : *"I get it, you're mad, the president mad, my Democratic friends are mad, my Republican friends are mad, my wife is mad, my kids are mad,even my dog is mad.. and Luka is a goldenDoodle,and they are never mad,we are all mad and when has it taken us, will a slipshod impeachment make us less mad or will it only give an invitation for the madness to follow in every future administration?"*

In this citation, we can see Jonathan at first seem to be told a solemn commentary, but after that, it is going to be less serious with a description of his dog's emotion this circumstance was turned to a lame commentary for a joke with the purpose of reducing the seriousness of this scandal, through it I consider that making a story become lame is a kind of art in-joke, in that speaker will tell a normal story but focus on unnecessary circumstances

## ART OF HUMOR

So, how can a lame story make people chuckle or smile? It relative to the program in our brain, commonly we used to hear a story having a good meaning, properly tale or circumstance,we consider it as the trail of rail track in our brain, for a lime story,it was pulled us out of that rail track, it lead to a result is an impression,and impression is the first reason why people smile with lame story, This technique also apply for movie industry, in particularly the episode travel Bean in mr Bean series, in the beginning sceneries, mr Bean go to his old car with a key was tied carefully to his belt by a long wire, it make audience think that is his car key,but not,it's just the key of car door, after opening his car door he took another key that was hidden under the car roof, that key then for opening the back bonnet,in the back bonnet he saw a wallet, he carefully open the wallet then he saw another key,this key then was took to open the front bonnet, after opening front bonnet he saw another key once again, this key right now is truly key of the car, Bean was very excited to start his car with this key, after so many steps of security,finally he can start his trip now,he put the key to ignition and twisted, the car rumble so loud but cannot run,it was out of gasoline, he got out his car with trouble on his face, he left it on the street then go to bus station..., in this circumstance, I recognize that some sceneries were created for fun as lame circumstances from the key was tied carefully to mr Bean belt as a trick to make audience thought his car is very important or maybe a luxury car,the period of discovering the truly car key is the main plot that unnecessary for it's complicated, it is lame and also it is the most costly sceneries in this series, lame stories are unnecessary But it is really attractive because of the difference, if you want to learn lame style,Jimmy Kimmel is the best teacher I recommend, after reading this book and watching his show, his speech we will easily realize it(lame style),and in the time when I started for writing this book,he had some best joke in oscar event in 2018 (talking with oscar statue on the stage), his show on YouTube " the handsome man club" it is exactly a statue in lime style joke also an art of using unnecessary things, turn it (youtube)on and you may learn something interesting from him, it's lame from the title to content, once again before finishing this part the rule of this joke is:

- *focus on unnecessary circumstances*

The next technique bring us to Russia, the biggest country in the world, also knowing as one of the funniest countries on earth with over thousand years of history, this country had a long time suffering from severe climate and political systems of dictatorship, maybe humor and vodka were born on this land to make its citizens live better, the Soviet joke from communist time, leader joke, political joke, vodka a kind of happy water was saved them from sadness and disappointing, they are not only good at the political joke and vodka drinking but also the common joke in their daily life also superb, I have heard about a family in Russia *"one day the son tries to ask his father and uncle for some advice for his future, he having two choices, Marry or joining Russia national army, his father then lifted a cup of vodka, finish it, he said: marry or joining the army? If you marry, my son! there's nothing left to say, but if you're joining army there are two instances might happen you are survive or you might be killed, if you are survive there's nothing left to say, but if you were killed, there are two instances might happen: you might be buried under the pine or might be buried under the poplar, if you were buried under the poplar there's nothing left to say, but if you were buried under the pine, there are two instances might happen: the pine wood might be cutted down for making pencil or paper, if it was used for pencils, there's nothing left to say, but if it were use for papers, there are two instances might happen: papers for book or papers for toilet, if the papers for books there is nothing left to say, but if the papers using for toilet roll , there are two instances might happen, toilet roll for men or toilet roll for women, if toilet roll for men there is nothing left to say,but if toilet roll for women there are two instances might happen: the toilet papers may use for wiping her front or the toilet papers may use for wiping her back, if she wiping her back there is nothing left to say but if she wiping her front there is no fucking different to marry someone!"* The story was uploaded as a video on the Internet with over thousand laugh icons, likes and comments, it proven that the story is attractive and really funny, it's similar to so many situations in the past I have saw and practiced, this technique is repeating one sentence for different situations, belonging to charming joke,we usually see this technique in the speech of famous person in that they don't have intention to make it funny,funny in this circumstance playing the role as side-effect such as the speech yes we can(Barack Obama), Make America great again (Donal Trump), I have a Dream (Martin Luther King)...etc, It depend on the purpose of speaker, if they want it funny the technique make it funnier, if they want it become solemnity, the technique will make it more solemnity, moreover it requires a good memory and the capable of coping with genetic circumstance in communication from others, the art of this joke type is creating the coincidence in communication but actually it already arranged in your mind before, for people good at this type of joke,it will automatically proving you as an interesting people,thus connecting peoples together tighter.

Another version of this joke is saying a particular sentence of other people then repeat it in many times in conversation for mocking them, this version is needed higher level than the last one, it's similar to Jujutsu a kind of martial art of Japan, it's philosophy is using opponent's force against them "whereby an opponent's attack is deflected using their momentum against them in order to arrest their movements then throw them or pin them with a technique, thus controlling the opponent" most people did not pay attention to it, because it seldom appears in conversation, actually it is an art in communication then we usually see it in cinema, for example, the Harry Potter series at the beginning of part II Harry Potter and the deathly hallows, some circumstances were considered as classic speeches, the scenery described a Goblin asking Harry about the Gryffindor sword :

- Goblin: *you're pretty unusual it is? How did you come by the sword?*

- Harry: *It's complicated! Why did Bellatrix Lestrage think it should be in her vault at Gringotts?*

- Goblin: *it's complicated!*

This technique is recommended for flirting someone in case of you using it skillfully, however, it depends on your communicated style suitable with it or not

- ***Repeating a specific speech for different situation***

The next technique brings us to another simple joke it seldom happens in conversation in reality, but if you learn it, it may create some funny dialogues in particular, also our brain is a great creature of god because sometimes the thing we have learned in the past suddenly dawned in mind when we need it, this type of joke is created for this function of the brain, the joke works effectively in case of someone asking you a long question then you just replied them with a very short answer, it will be more effective if you replied it with a concise answer with full meaning for it own question, in Asia most father usually ask his prospective groom about his capable of taking care of his daughter before marrying, if the groom not having a good living condition, the wedding may not be allowed, there is an instance like:

- Father: *so you don't have money, no car, no home, jobless, how can you take care of my daughter, what do you have now?*

- Guy: *her pregnancy, sir!*

This example, definitely a joke, but the technique was used in this tale is the main factor of creating the funny things, if the guy replies with the same length to father's question, it's not a joke anymore

- **Answer short for the long question**

The next technique will teach us to be a man with bad behavior, commonly treating to a skinflint we seem to be annoyed with their lazy or scary in spending money, in reality this nastiness was performed on television series for satirizing it, children were touch to avoid it,this nastiness was seen as saving money as much as possible such as bring an apple to supermarket then go to knife shop for peeling it only, or trying to be rich by saving unnecessary things,although it is a nastiness but if we perform to audience for joke, it work effectively, from the ancient time to now,it's etymology still unknowingly, The theory of skinflint (very mean person) is skin a flint may come from the meaning skin a flea to eat it,seem to be disgusting explanation but describing with full meaning,then pretend to be a skinflint in a moment may mock the audience, sometime it may make people feeling disgusting(intention), it is the art of this joke, there are some tips of performing this nastiness to other people for mocking them such as:

- *pretending of saving money to minimum digit*

We can see it popular in comedy or television series, The main actor count money penny to penny for donation or counting to the last penny to buy something

- ***Saving the little thing to being rich one day***

Each people having their own dream and the dream of being rich is unexceptional, in a beautiful day if your buddy tells you that he can not go out for party because he has to save his money for buying his apartment, trust me, it is a joke, it exactly the joke I'm mentioning to, however, there is an exception in this joke, in case of misunderstanding you are real skinflint because you're too successful in this joke, and the drama needs to end with *"I'm just kidding"*

The final type of joke i want to show you in this book located as the highest level, hard to perform also hard to describe this process, I call it as a process because of it's complicated essential by it self, it require you to know yourself well and a little skill of acting, i'm talking about the process of breaking your own image, this process is recognizing your image then your joke is putting you to opposite image, for explaining it more clearly we got a pair of examples: old man/baby, if you are an old man,your joke is acting like a baby: laughing,playing or having the same hobbies to them,i mean do the things that only baby do,and if you are a young person,do the contrary things, so please don't misunderstand me that you are always have to do this process for joke, in particularly this joke will work effectively only once for one any person or one any group, if you do it in the second time it will be less effectively than the first one, there is a circumstance of breaking image, it was happened in 2007 in a meeting of two famous leadership of the world,Angela Merkel and Vladimir Putin,the meeting seem to be solemnity in their negotiation, then suddenly a big black dog of

Putin ran into their room and she sniffed Merkel, it make her froze and frightened in a moment,trouble on her face and her majesty gone with the wind because of her fear in the past that she had been bitten in 1995, what a sad memory of her,however it is a lively example for this joke that easier for your imagination,an example seem to be funny but when we think twice about it,it seem to be nothing funny anymore because of it serious essential by it self, also it seem to be the negotiation was collapsed after that, because two of them haven't meet with each other anymore, for a long time!

- *putting you to opposite image*

In the end of this book, I would like wishing you, the readership reading this book luckily, happiness and longevity with a smile on your lips always, also wishing the people on your way of discovery your humor spirit inside you, a hope of better future with the most suitable joke style in this book, i hope the next authors, next generations after reading this book will improve it, inherit it thus I will not feeling lonely on the way of making this world happier, if you find the joke style suitable with you but haven't succeeded in communication, don't be sad, practice makes perfect, at last, to finish this book I would like to send you a famous quote from a famous person:

"It is common sense to take a method and try it, if it fails, admit it frankly and try another, but above all, try something"

Good luck to you, the man traveling on the adventure to become an interesting people

God bless you!

## CHAPTER III: FIDDLE-FADDLE

it's me again!

My book may have finished in 2 last chapter but when I check it again I thought I need something to say but there's no space to talk about it, also my books need to be thicker to not make you disappointed because of it's length, indeed I may feeling sad if this book cannot help you anything from a chuckle, it is my biggest nightmare! anyway, I hope it will be better than the famous book from Cindy Cashman "everything Men know about women" This book will spell out some topics such as making friends with women, romancing with women, satisfying women... Etc even though this book is completely blank, The author recommend giving it to your girlfriend if you want a laugh from her with the price around five dollars, Obviously my book have much more words than hers

## SOME BASIC ADVISE

- So many people may consider humor belong to emotion, it's not true humor belong to rational thinking and making a joke is a skill of controlling other emotion,we have seen so many comedians in the world success with their joke with out laughing by their own joke until their audiences laugh ,it's rational thinking,it was shown with the capable of pretending to be serious, controlling their own emotion to not be laugh first, it similar to a professional guitarist performing in concert eventhough the song they are playing animated or not they still feeling calm with guitar on their hands,it belong to the skills they have learned in the past, thanks to that,they can stay out of their own emotion and playing music with skill and reason in front of thousand audiences,now you understand why a professional funny person never laugh with his own trick, and learning how to making a joke from someone and do it by your own way to be successful is easier than learning to play a guitar,There are some misunderstand in reading this book such as somebody may think after learning some basic rule of humor you will become funnier, that's only exactly in case of you have a little sense of humor first, for a person have no sense of humor it will be harder, your own mind at first need to be improved to become more generous, creating space in your mind to realize something funny something not, if you can not change your mind maybe this book is not so suitable for you,more over watching comedy shows have the same effect

- You should not always try to joke in communication after reading this book, forcing yourself to be a funny man may lead to stressful, remember humor is the spice of communication, let it be natural,also picking style of joke that most suitable with you and make it become your nature, your brain will program it automatically, you will become better every single day when you try to practice it by recognizing which type of humor surrounding you then your mission after this book firstly is keeping calm and think twice about what is the type suitable most with you, practicing it becomes perfect to make someone chuckle first is the priority, hard practicing always bringing something legend, it refers to a quote of Bruce Lee a martial art star "I fear not the man who has practiced 10,000 kicks once, but I fear the man who has practiced one kick 10,000 times"

- Even though dirty mind joke is a popular and effective way for a joke I still recommend you to do it fewer and using it with generous people, to be rash in dirty joke will become a disaster and leading to some unpredictable consequences, anyway joke with your heart always better

- Despite humor having so many more styles and some of them cannot be described in writing or verbal such as playing words...etc

I hope it will bring a new point of views to you in this field, and because of my desire to make this book become an international book of humor and from it so many people can learn it and apply it to reality, even though the difference of culture and language are barriers but humor is ideas

HUMAN ESSENTIAL

From the ancient time, human having an essential, it's always trying to find something funny and avoiding boring things in their whole life, there's nothing changed until now, this is the reason why most of boring books published in 20 century have fallen in turnover, and the entertainment industry developed in steadily, children need toys in their childhood and when they growing adult,they still need toys,but different toys, nowadays with industrial lifestyle, people living with rush, money and stressful it's harder to smile or laugh with this environment, The reason why life quality become worse when they having much money more but less smile and time, It create developed conditions for some exercise to laugh or educating for laugh,the example is laughter Yoga, in this kind of exercise, you will pay money for teacher of the club (laughter club),just only for learning to laugh, It's sound stupid but true story!, in this club students will learn how to laugh with different techniques, different level,laugh with your eyes or any part on your body,original from India in the mid 90s today it is become more developed and popular in the world and if you are living in sadness ,boring or finding something interesting,this exercise is recommended.

Not only laugh club but also something can make people feeling funny to have become a tool in every field in the purpose of attracting other people, especially in the fashion industry, we can see the T-shirt with interesting messages always become Best selling products, it was made with different types of humor such as:

- *Trending speech:*

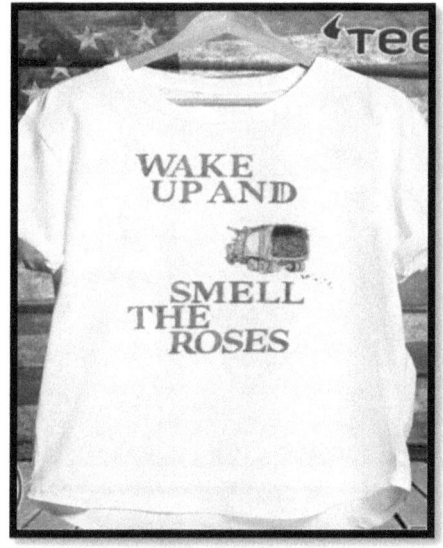

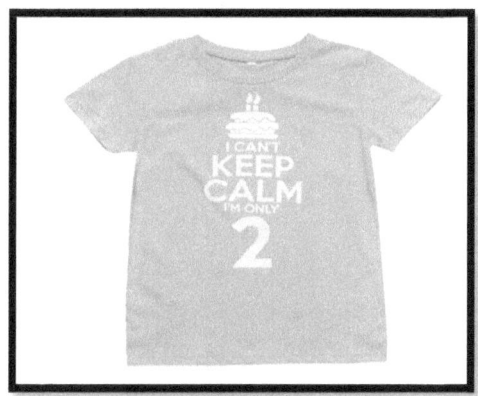

- *Breaking image*

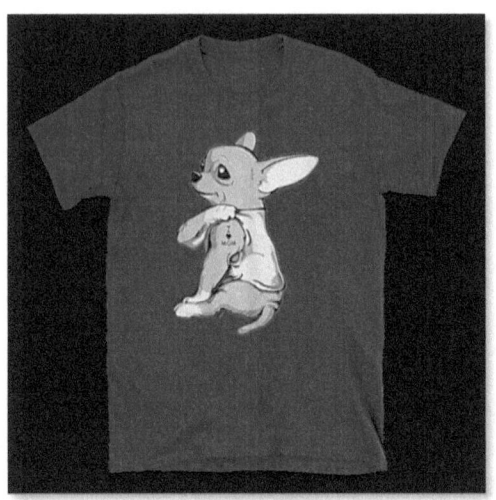

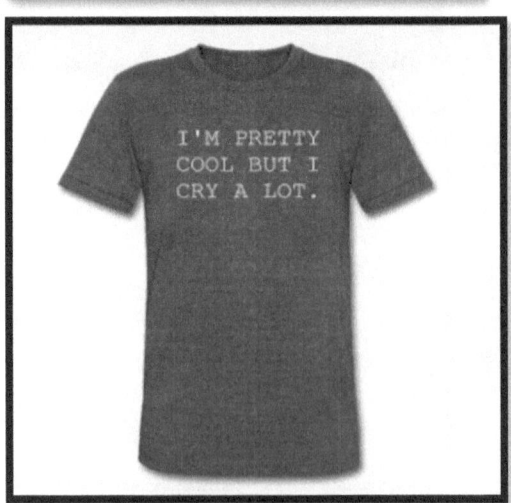

- *Comparison*

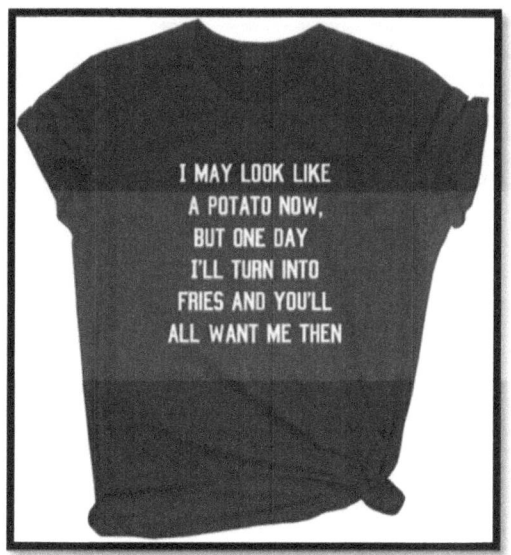

(This T-shirt not for skinny people)

- *Implication:*

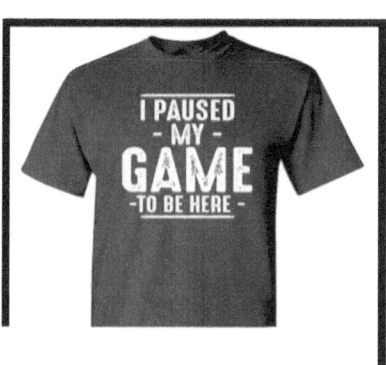

Not only fashion but also pub and coffee shop

- *Dirty way of joke:*

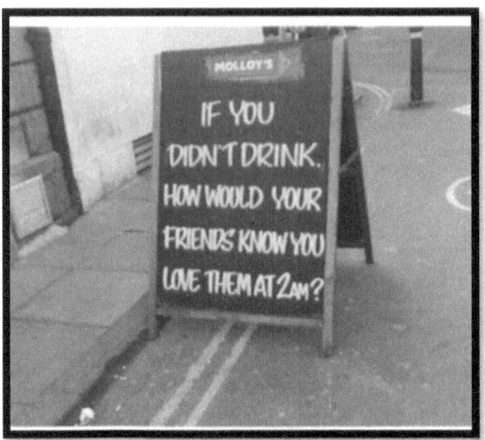

*Comparison:*

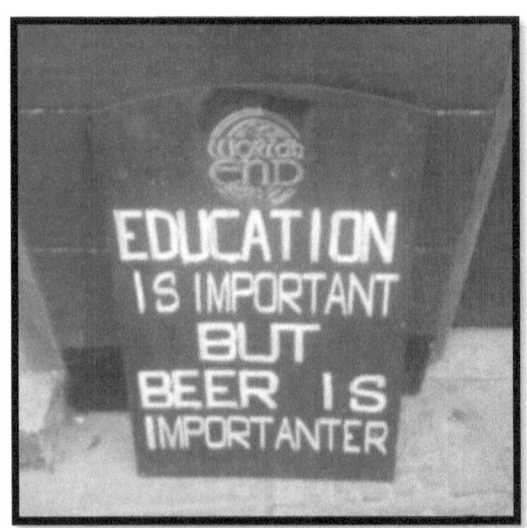

- *Implication:*

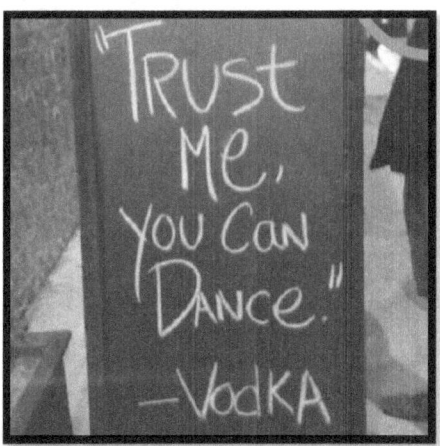

BENEFIT OF SMILING

They are so many research the world has found out benefits of smiling such as:

- Smiling make you younger when we smile or laugh so stressed from facial muscle, head and neck Stretch, make you look younger than a man always in seriousness

- Smiling will improve your working efficiency studies have shown that smiling or laughing has its own good to working efficiency, A positive mood may allow an employee solving their in creation, more energy and capable of passing challenge and working pressure are higher

- Smiling make you longevity: The combination of benefits in smiling have shown that it can make people longevity, there are some research has proven smiling can make a person live seven years longer than others

- Smiling reducing medical fee, there are some doctors in Japan have supplied to an old man club a program of healthcare with exercise and lab practicing, about 92% of them have a report that they medical have reduced 30%

- More attractive: Studies have shown that smiling will Increase attractive in an associate that you will become more friendly if you have a good sense of humor, in a famous book "how to win friends and influence people" it has a rule, the rule said that " let's smile" your smiling bring happiness to all the people who surround you, also happy to yourself

- Reducing pain: Study from Oxford University have recognized that smile play an important role in pain endurance by releasing endorphins

- Improving your sleep: Japan researchers have found out that smiling at night will encouraging human body releasing melatonin

- Improving your heart: Study from Maryland university had proven the relationship between a person who used to smile every day, researchers have found out that the person who has heart disease smile fewer 40% done same age person with no heart disease, otherwise smiling will improve blood circulation and reducing the risk of stroke and heart disease

- Increasing HGH: researchers in Loma University discovered that smiling a lot will make human body increase HGH (an anti-aging) to 87%, It is the reason why a person with a good sense of humor always seems to be younger than others whom always staying in trouble and seriousness

- Reducing stress: The people who used to smile every day are optimists and smiling is the way to have a lower level of stressful

HUMOR AND LOVE

Making a funny joke as a first impression in flirting always proven is effectively, and if it succeeds, of course, in any situation it is the best way to attract some mate or naturally start your friendship, it makes other people feeling more comfortable with each other, also creating the basis for understanding with each other, following some studies, improving some benefits of humor such as:

- making the Tighter relationship: when someone tries to make a joke the last for purpose is trying to make someone laugh, it makes our spiritual health better, Especially on the bed, some studies said that a human person can make they mate feel orgasm easier than other, this not only true in reality but also true in the novel, the character Jamesbond can handle Bond girls, by chance gentleman also love to make love with a funny girl on bed Than other who always in serious

- A colorful lifestyle: loving a funny person may make the whole life unpredictable and drama with his Characteristic, people said that " A leopard cannot change its spot" because A funny person always knows how to make his life never boring

- A healthy life: A funny person always brings his optimistic energy everywhere he visits, also for his sweetheart, with his funny all the things boring or pessimistic things Will stay far away you, less angry, less disagreement also leading to less alcoholic

## HUMOROUS TOOLS

-Blaming in humor: life is not always peaceful sometimes we may have a conflict with someone, sometime we need to blame them sometimes not, it depends on the capacity of your emotional controlling, and blaming someone is really an art if you blame someone and make them change their mind without making them angry, so if blaming is an art blamer should be an artist, in this case, blamer need to have a warm heart and kindness with the last purpose "make someone change but not make them angry " the most popular way is pretending to be a person in anger but blaming in gentle language, rational language! Of course, it is not easy to change someone's mind but blaming with real anger only make everything worse, otherwise losing emotional controlling may lead to violence, however, if blaming in humor successfully, you will reduce the frustration from others, at least it will make no one hurt whenever conflict happen.

-presentation: So many people in the world afraid of speaking in front of a crowd, especially in presentation, when you have to stand in front of a group of audience and talk about something you don't like, it similar to stay in the hell, for this case, humor is a cool tool for improving your situation! using humor rules to your presentation always appreciated by audiences who watching you second by second on the stage, for this case humor playing a role as natural caffeine that help other audiences feeling not sleepy with a very long presentation and boring subjects, it also playing a role of attracting people pay attention to your speech, importantly it will get rid of your stress in a solemn room

-making friends: making friends! for some people it has become a legend skill, especially for a person that working in a multilevel marketing company, but in here I'm not telling you to do it like them, humor in making friend, it playing a role of catalysis that may make you become friend with someone or make someone hate you at the first meet, I am mentioning to the law of attraction, basically, this law said that something similar with each other, it will attract with each other, humor is positive energy inside you, if you meet someone who has a little positive energy, you all will become friend with each other, otherwise, someone doesn't have that positive energy they may far away you, indeed your character is a filter of friendship, in communication humor playing a role of making the first impression to someone, if you can do all the rules in this book effectively, from this moment your filter starts working

-Stop making argument

In any argument, especially argument to your life partner, there is a funny method to finish your argument(nonsense argument) with the priority condition you should be a generous person with good emotional controlling, commonly argument will happen when people become meltdown without tolerance, it will bring the relationship to knife-edge,worse it will collapse, so what would we do with it? to find out the solution, we should understand more about it, usually, when argument happens, it combines insulting, swearing, blaming without reason..., they are the factors that may lead to a bad consequence in any relationship, for a more clear explanation of this method, we will see an example of an argument from a couple :

-Women: *you are bastard, you're cheating me*

-Men: *shut up! I'm tired of you*

-Women: *Go to hell now, asshole!*

-Men: *@$#@!#@$#%...*

In this dialogue both of them are losing emotional controlling, one of them is in crazy status, and one of them tired, but if the men good at emotional controlling, generous and apply the funny method to an argument, everything will change, below there is the same dialogue but in case of applying the funny method:

-Women: you are bastard, you're cheating me

-Men: *yes I'm bastard Honey, sit down and tell me why?*

-Women: *Go to hell now, asshole!*

-Men: *OK, honey I will go to hell now...*

I guess in the second dialogue the couple will finish with a happy ending, from the example we can see the method is simply with listening to the blamer, agree to blamer and admit all the things they say are right, especially keep calm in any situation, from the example as long as the men good at emotional controlling and answer in calm, the argument will finish when the striker too tired because no one against her, and the final step is talk in peace with reason, this method will work effectively in case of people in nonsense argument and you are a victim of blamer, if you apply this method you should listen and agree in seriousness, otherwise the victim do this method with smiling everything will become worse

## HOW TO SUCESS FROM CHUCKLE WITH THIS BOOK

1. Making a joke is a skill in communication, when we talk let's it be natural,don't try to joke if you cannot joke, I don't have the intention to make you become a comedian, my advice is learning the rules and just relax

2. There is an important request to you, the readership reading this book, the priority is a desire of changing your mind, an open mind to receive all new knowledges, formula or humor rules..., it is from that, you can make a massive change in you, and make you better every day than ever, There is a quote, it said that " every day when I wake up I hope I'll be better than yesterday" and on the road to happiness or beauty in your spirit, this desire is indispensable, it is an important thing you have to do, if you can't, this book only for entertainment!

3. Reading in the digest is the second important factor to change your mind, art of humor with concise literary style and enormous meaning with an intention of making sure that you will not feel boring with many times reading this book, again and again, then every time you read it, you will find the new things with interesting when you apply it to reality, otherwise Reading this book until you cannot laugh anymore with funny stories in this book, reading slowly and digest is the best method to understand well all the humor rules, all the rules in the book had been experienced and it is so pity when you read it in skimming

4. For making it become a practiced book, I recommend you to prepare a highlight pen (or note), when you reading this book it will highlight stories you like, also highlights the most humor style that suitable with you, I believe that you will find some interesting things and experience every time you lift this book and open it

5. Learning by practicing is a deciding factor to make someone laugh, this book was designed for practicing in reality, if you cannot apply, your knowledge gonna die in vain, you cannot swim if you read a swimming book and imagine you are swimming, even literally style of this book including by it own humor rules

6. After applying it(humor rules) to reality, The important step to make you better is self-examination this step will help you improve your skill in-joke, finding out something right something wrong and ask yourself the question: if the time turns back to the past that circumstance happened once again will I still behaving like before? What I have learned from it?

7. Using all the methods you are owning such as A notebook to note your experiences, fail jokes of you or your friends, what comedy teach you in-joke... if you can do it, I'm sure you will become better every day, if you success, Center of every party or

surrounded by the most seductive people are your best awards...moreover winning over your self.

In conclusion for turning your communication method into entertainment style:

- I desire development in-joke skill and controlling your own emotion in communication

- when you reading this book, sometime you should stop in paragraph, humor rules and asking yourself how to apply these things to reality

- Highlight the content you like

- Every weekend take a short time for checking your notebook and remind all the things you have did, realizing anything you did funny or not

- Writing down date, time or moment you have applied it to reality,

and think twice about your fault in joke

8. Art of Humor is not a book for teaching in communication, it shows you a higher level in communication(making a joke), it is will be more effective in reading this book if you learn some skill in communication for the communicational platform before, in this case, the book How to win friends and influence people-Dale Carnegie is recommended

www.ingramcontent.com/pod-product-compliance
Lightning Source LLC
Chambersburg PA
CBHW030649220526
45463CB00005B/1695